THE ROSETTA STONE

STEPHEN SLOAN

Artesian **Press**

P.O. Box 355, Buena Park, CA 90621
www.artesianpress.com

Nonfiction
Ancient Egyptian Mystery Series

Cover photo courtesy the Rosicrucian Egyptian Museum, San Jose, California
Project Editor: Molly Mraz
Illustrator: Fujiko
Graphic Design: Tony Amaro
©2004 Artesian Press

 Artesian **Press**

ISBN 1-58659-209-2

CONTENTS

Word List

Abercromby (AB-ur-crahm-bee), **Sir Ralph** The general of the British army when the Rosetta Stone was found.

Alexandria (al-ihg-ZAN-dree-uh) A famous city near the Nile River in Egypt.

Bonaparte, Napoleon (BO-nuh-part, nuh-POE-lee-uhn) The great general who led the French army and conquered Egypt in 1798. Napoleon began to search for the forgotten language of the ancient Egyptians.

Cairo (KIE-roh) One of Egypt's ancient capital cities, along with Alexandria.

cartouche (kar-TOOSH) An oval or oblong shape used to enclose the name of an ancient Egyptian.

Champollion (shahn-poe-LEEON), **Jean François** A Frenchman who studied the Rosetta Stone and made discoveries about how to read hieroglyphics.

Coptic (KOP-tik) A language of ancient Egypt.

demotic (dih-MAHT-ihk) The cursive writing of ancient Egypt, which was a popular way to write.

delta (DEL-tuh) The wide end of a river where soil is deposited.

hieroglyphics (hie-ruh-GLIFF-iks) The religious writing of ancient Egypt.

Menou (men-OO), **Jacques-François** A general of the French army when the Rosetta Stone was found.

pictograph (PIK-tuh-graf) A picture that represents an idea.

Ptolemy (TAHL-uh-mee) The general that ruled Egypt after Alexander the Great conquered.

Ptolemy V (TAHL-uh-mee) A ruler of Egypt who was so popular that the Egyptians carved a message about him into the Rosetta Stone.

Rameses (RAM-eh-seez) One of the most famous Egyptian Pharaohs.

Rashid (rah-SHEED) A city in Egypt to the north of Alexandria.

Rosetta (roe-ZET-uh) The new name for the city of Rashid.

Rosetta Stone A big black stone with a message about Ptolemy V carved on it in three languages.

Turner, Colonel (KUR-nuhl) The British officer in charge of sending the Rosetta Stone and other important French discoveries back to London.

Young, Thomas A British man who studied the Rosetta Stone and helped to translate its demotic writing.

Chapter 1

Reading can be exciting! Learning to read can sometimes be hard, but it is worth the effort. The world's best stories are just waiting to be read.

Imagine that some of these great stories were written in a language that no one--not even the smartest person in the world--could read. This actually happened. Until 1821, no one could read the ancient Egyptian language. The smartest people in the world tried and tried, but they couldn't figure it out. The knowledge was lost!

For hundreds of years, people missed out on hearing the exciting stories of ancient Egypt--its powerful armies, generals, and Pharaohs. No one knew about Egypt's enemies or that the people believed the Pharaoh, or king, was a god. They didn't know why or how the huge stone pyramids were built. But the Egyptians *wanted* people to know their history. They wrote their stories down and even carved them in stone thousands of years ago.

All of these stories would stay lost until someone could figure out how to read the Egyptian writing. Scientists got some help when a large stone was found with a message carved on it in three different languages. Scientists already knew how to read one of the languages, and they guessed that the message said the same thing in all three languages. They thought they could figure out how to read the languages they didn't know by using the language they *did* know. It was like breaking a code. If they were right, they could break the code and finally read the amazing stories of an ancient people!

Chapter 2

The Nile River divides into many smaller rivers at its northern end. The wide end is called a *delta*. In ancient times, there were many cities along the Nile's delta. One famous city was Alexandria (a-lig-ZAN-dree-uh). Another city, Rashid (rah-SHEED), was to the north of Alexandria on a smaller river.

Rashid was a small town of hard-working farmers. They grew enough food to feed their families and sell some to people in other cities. They used cattle and oxen for food, to pull wagons, or to sell to other people. The people of Rashid made money and built a small temple to the gods of ancient Egypt.

Over the years, Egypt's government

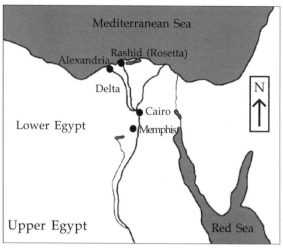

This map of Egypt shows the location of Rashid, where the Rosetta Stone was found.

changed. The capital city was moved from one place to another. The powerful families that controlled the government also changed. As other nations became more powerful, they fought and beat Egypt's armies. Then they took over Egypt's government.

In 331 B.C., about 2,300 years ago, the Greek general Alexander the Great conquered Egypt. About eight years later, the Greek general Ptolemy (TAHL-uh-mee) became the ruler of Egypt. Many generations of Greek-Egyptian rulers came from the same family and used the name *Ptolemy*.

There were many changes in the lives of the Egyptians when the Greeks took over the country. One of the changes was the way people wrote. The language of the new rulers was Greek, not Egyptian. From the time that Alexander took over Egypt, all official writing was done in Greek. This was a big change. All of the important papers had to be written in Greek and all the words on buildings had to be in Greek.

Since the writing in Egypt had already changed many times, this change in writing did not make much difference to most of the people. They did not know how to

General Alexander the Great took over Egypt.

©1995–2003 Douglas Hackney

read or write anyway, so it did not affect their daily lives. But well-educated Egyptians who worked in the government or had important jobs needed to understand the new laws that were written in Greek.

As the Greeks took over Egypt and influenced its culture, the ancient Egyptian languages were forgotten. Part of Egypt's history could have been a mystery forever without the little temple that the people of Rashid built a long time ago.

How could an old temple, buried in the sand in a forgotten city, help people understand the ancient land of Egypt? What secrets did it have for scientists to find thousands of years later?

Chapter 3

Ptolemy V became the ruler of Egypt about 2,200 years ago. After his rule, a group of priests wanted to tell the world about him. Their message was carved in stone and put in many public places for people to read.

In the tiny temple at Rashid, the message was carved into a hard black stone. It was written in ancient Egypt's cursive writing (which means the letters are joined) called *demotic* (dih-MAH-tik). *Demotic* is a Greek word that means "popular." Most ancient Egyptians wrote this way. The message was then written in Greek so everyone could read the information.

Then the message was written a third

In the tiny temple at Rashid, the message was carved into a hard black stone in three different languages.

time, in the ancient religious writing called *hieroglyphics* (hie-ruh-GLIFF-iks). *Hieroglyphics* is not an Egyptian word. It is a Greek word that means "sacred carvings." That is what the Greeks called the ancient Egyptian writing system. At the time, very few people could write or read hieroglyphics.

At the temple in Rashid, only one man, an old priest, could use the writing. It was an honor for the priest to be asked to write the message in the beautiful old hieroglyphics.

The work was slow and hard. Each word had to be cut into stone with a sharp chisel that was hit with a hammer. Some of the letters and signs were circles or pictures of animals. The priest held the chisel in his left hand and hit it with a hammer held in his right hand. It was easier for him to work from right to left.

The stone used was a beautiful black stone. It was 6 feet tall. From side to side, it was almost 2.5 feet wide. It was 11 inches thick. The stone was very heavy. It weighed almost three quarters of a ton, or about 1,500 pounds.

The writing on the stone looked beautiful when it was finished. The 6-foot stone with the message stood behind a small statue of Ptolemy V. The statue was painted to look like a live person. It was covered with clothes and was treated as if it were a god.

The finished message and the statue stood in the temple for many years. During that time, many changes took place in Egypt. Egypt's government and religion changed many more times. The temple at Rashid got old and was rebuilt. Many of the statues were taken out of the temple. The walls needed to be repaired. Some of the stones in the temple were used to fix the walls. The big, heavy, black stone with the carved message about Ptolemy V was one of the stones used to repair a wall.

More time passed, and the temple was no longer used. Years became centuries, and the old temple at Rashid was forgotten. It was broken--nothing was left standing. The black stone with the message was buried deep under the ground, covered by dirt and sand.

Would anybody ever see the black

stone again? Who would be able to read the words and names carved into it?

In 1798, the French army, led by the great general Napoleon Bonaparte (neh-POE-lee-ehn BONE-uh-part), fought and conquered Egypt. French scientists began to discover many ancient temples and monuments with writing that no one could read.

But if nobody understood the ancient language of the Egyptians, who would be able to read the writings from so long ago? How would anyone figure out the code of symbols used in the writings? Where were the clues to solve the mystery? They didn't know that the answers were right under their feet.

Chapter 4

The city of Rashid did not exist anymore. After many centuries, it was called Rosetta (roe-ZET-uh). It was not an important city in Egypt in 1798. However, it was in an important place. It was near a river that connected the Mediterranean Sea with the Nile River. From the place south of Rosetta where the two rivers met, it was easy to get to Cairo (KIE-roh), one of Egypt's capital cities. Cairo was one of many cities where important things happened. The two most important Egyptian cities were Cairo and Alexandria.

Much had happened in Egypt since the big black stone was carved in the temple at Rashid. In the many years that passed, the Egyptian language changed. The writings on the temples and the tombs of the people who lived so long ago became a mystery to all the people of the world. Nobody could understand the writings or the language. How did this happen?

As the many changes happened in the world, the rulers of Egypt changed, too. Some rulers had new languages and new ways of writing. People forgot how to read the ancient languages. First, the hieroglyphics were forgotten. Then the spoken language changed so much that the meaning of the writing was lost. The last time that hieroglyphics were officially carved was in A.D. 394. Then the cursive writing of demotic was replaced with Arabic languages used by the people who took over Egypt. Demotic was last written in A.D. 452.

The final form of Egyptian writing was called Coptic (KOP-tik). It was the spoken and written language of Christians in Egypt. Today, that same written language is used in the Coptic Church.

In the sixth century, Arabic became the language of Egypt. It is still the language of most of Egypt's people today.

If the ancient languages of Egypt were lost, how were they found? How can we read them now? The big black stone in Rashid was an important key to help us understand the ancient Egyptians.

In 1798, Napoleon sailed to Egypt with 35,000 French soldiers. They had to sail around British ships in the Mediterranean Sea. Napoleon did it safely.

The famous French general Napoleon conquered Egypt.

They attacked the Turks, who controlled Egypt at that time. At the Battle of the Pyramids, the French beat the Turkish army. Napoleon became the general in charge of Egypt, the way Alexander the Great had been before him.

The French built a new fort near Rashid, called Fort Julien, to help defend themselves against the British. Fort Julien was built right next to the old temple of Rashid. But by then, the old temple was just a pile of forgotten dirt and stones.

The French victory did not last long. In 1799, British ships attacked and defeated French ships in the sea battle of the Nile. Soon, British armies landed on the ground to fight against the French.

Napoleon knew he was in big trouble. He could not get the war supplies he needed because British ships were in his way. He could not beat the British armies and the new Turkish armies.

All the ancient things that the French found in Egypt could be lost if the British defeated them. When Napoleon took over

Napoleon's troops paraded at Rosetta.

the country, he began to study its ancient monuments. He started a school to study everything in Egypt. He thought that if he knew about the country, he could be a better ruler and keep things peaceful.

Napoleon invited artists, doctors, historians, and many kinds of scientists from France to study in Egypt. They described, identified, and made a written record of everything that was found. If the British defeated the French, all of the school's hard work would be lost. So the French soldiers were ready to fight the British.

The French decided to make the walls of Fort Julien bigger and stronger. On a hot July day in 1799, the commander of the fort told the lieutenant to take some men and find bricks to expand the fort.

The lieutenant and soldiers went outside to look for the materials the Egyptians had used to make buildings. They gathered bricks from several old buildings and took them back to the fort. In the afternoon, they dug up the wall of an old building, and one soldier's shovel hit a hard rock. The soldiers began to dig the dirt away from around the stone. As they dug, they saw writing on the front of the stone.

They worked quickly to move away the dirt. They could see that the stone was finely carved. On part of the stone, they saw the beautiful, ancient Egyptian religious writing. Below that, they could see cursive demotic writing. Even further below that, they could see the writing of ancient Greece. They found the black stone with the message about Ptolemy!

None of the men could read any of the old writing, but they knew right away that they were looking at something important. They did not yet know how important the big black stone really was, but they knew that they had to get it back to the fort quickly.

The big stone was no longer in one piece. Over the many years, the carved stone had been broken into pieces. It was not 6 feet tall anymore. Now it was only 3 feet 9 inches tall. Some of the top was broken off, and part of the bottom was broken. The soldiers could see that some of the words were missing from both the hieroglyphics at the top and the Greek at the sides and the bottom.

The lieutenant realized that he had found something very valuable. By studying the three languages together, maybe scientists could begin to figure out how to read the ancient languages on the stone.

After the soldiers took the stone back to the fort, the officers there decided to send the stone from Fort Julien, near the town of Rosetta, to the French school in Cairo, so the people there could study it. The officers told General Menou (men-OO), chief of the French army, about the stone. He ordered them to bring it from Rosetta to Cairo. Since the stone was found near the city of Rosetta, they called it the Rosetta Stone.

Chapter 5

The Rosetta Stone arrived in Cairo at the same time that the British army arrived in Egypt. At the famous French school in Cairo, language experts began to study the writing on the Rosetta Stone. They could read the ancient Greek writing. Many educated people during the 1700s could read Greek and Latin well. The language experts were sure that the message in each of the languages was the same. They knew this because the last part of the message told the Egyptian priest to write the same message in three languages: two Egyptian languages and Greek.

This was the scientists' first big hint, and they were very excited. The next problem was to discover a way to find out the exact words of the other two languages. They had to work on it as if it were a secret code. What they needed was a key that would help them figure out the code of the two ancient languages.

The scientists had two ways of thinking about the ancient hieroglyphics. One way was to think of each picture as being one word, sentence, or idea. This meant that a picture of a hawk, for example, stood for one single idea. Three different pictures, then, were three complete ideas. That is true in the writing of some cultures, where a picture called a *pictograph* (PIK-toe-graf) represents an idea. For example, in Chinese, the sign 人 means *man* or *person*. It shows one idea as one pictograph.

Another way to think about the writing was that each picture was a sound, and many sounds made up words. So to make the word *man*, for example, pictures of things with the sounds of *m, a,* and *n* were put together. Each picture was like a letter of the alphabet.

The Greek writing on the Rosetta Stone used the ancient Greek alphabet. That is why the people who knew that ancient alphabet could read the Greek message on the stone. But what did the demotic and the hieroglyphics sound like? Nobody could speak the old languages. How would they know if the written language was an alphabet or a series of pictographs?

An even bigger problem was that they needed more scientists to look at the Rosetta Stone. If the stone could be sent to France, scientists and university teachers could look at it and think about how to solve the mystery. But the British ships and army were there to stop the French scientists from sending the Rosetta Stone back to France. The war between the French and the British made that impossible.

At last, someone had the idea to try to use the stone like a printing plate. The entire surface of the stone was covered with ink. But the ink could not cover the carved words because they were cut below the surface of the rock.

Once the ink was on the surface of the stone, large sheets of paper were put over the top, and rubber rollers were pushed back and forth on the back of the paper. When the paper was taken off the stone, the carved words were white on the paper because no ink had touched them, but the flat part of the stone was black on the paper from the ink. After the ink dried, the paper could be folded and copies would be sent to different scientists in other parts of the world.

Time was getting short. The British army was landing on the coast of Egypt. The army began to march toward Cairo. Sir Ralph Abercromby (AB-ur-crahm-bee) was the general of the British army. The French general, Menou, wanted to save the Rosetta Stone for France before Abercromby arrived.

General Menou thought he had a good

Sir Ralph Abercromby was the general of the British army when the French found the Rosetta Stone.

idea. Since General Abercromby was marching to Cairo, why not send the Rosetta Stone to Alexandria? Menou had a house in Alexandria, and he figured he could hide the stone there until the battle was over. That way, even if the British army won, the stone would stay with the French. It seemed like a good idea, so the general ordered that the Rosetta Stone be moved to his home in Alexandria at once.

He wanted it out of Cairo before the British army arrived.

The scientists did not have time to finish studying the Rosetta Stone before it had to leave Cairo, but they could look at the large paper prints of the words and symbols on the stone.

They began their study. They were still trying to figure out which of the two ways, pictograph or alphabet, they could use to read the messages on the stone. They noticed that some of the pictures in the hieroglyphics were inside long circles. What could that mean?

Chapter 6

The Rosetta Stone was safe in Alexandria by the time the British army arrived in Cairo. Most of the French scientists stayed in Cairo with the other treasures that the French found in Egypt. They made many discoveries of Egyptian art, tombs, and scrolls of writing, and they made many notes about their discoveries.

When the British army arrived in Cairo, they saw all the hard work that the French had done. In the agreement that ended the war, the British let the French scientists keep all the discoveries they made that were in Cairo. The British knew that the French scientists worked very hard on the ancient Egyptian treasures. They let the French send everything back to France for more study, but anything that was not in Cairo would belong to the British.

Where was the Rosetta Stone? It was in Alexandria. If the French had left it in Cairo, it would have been theirs to keep as part of the agreement. To keep it safe, they had moved it out of Cairo, which meant they had lost it to the British.

However, the British did not yet have it. The British officer in charge of sending French discoveries back to London was Colonel (KER-nuhl) Turner. He was a very careful man. He made a list of everything that was put on the two ships to be sent to England. He knew how important it was to find the Rosetta Stone.

Every day, Colonel Turner checked the work of his soldiers to see if the Rosetta Stone was put on one of the ships. No one ever saw it. Colonel Turner learned that the Rosetta Stone was not in the warehouse with the other discoveries. He began to wonder where it might be hidden.

Because General Menou kept the Rosetta Stone with his own personal belongings, this became a serious problem for both the British and the French. If the British officers complained to the French officers that General Menou was keeping the Rosetta Stone, it would be an insult to the French army. If the British officers did *not* complain to the French army, General Menou would take the Rosetta Stone to France. If there was a complaint, there might be more fighting between the two armies and more soldiers would die. Was a big stone worth the lives of more men?

Colonel Turner had an idea. He decided to get British historians to help bring back the Rosetta Stone. By doing this, the army would not take the chance of going to war again. He knew that there were French and British historians visiting the city of Alexandria, and they all knew each other. It was better to let the historians solve the problem and to keep the army out of it.

Colonel Turner asked the British historians to visit him one day. He told them how important the missing stone was and where he thought the stone was being kept. Turner knew that they would talk to the French historians. Nobody wanted to go to war over the Rosetta Stone.

On April 23, 1803, on a very dark, quiet street in the city of Alexandria, three British historians met three French historians in the middle of the night. They all shook hands and talked quietly. There were no other people on the small street.

Soon they heard the sound of horses coming toward them. The horses were pulling a wagon that was loaded with something heavy. The heavy object was covered with cloth. The wagon came close to the six men standing in the dark street. It slowed and stopped in front of them.

The driver of the wagon got down from the cart and saluted the three French historians. Then he walked away from the wagon. From around the corner, two

British soldiers ran to the wagon and climbed up to the driver's seat. They drove the wagon to the end of the street and turned back toward the direction from which they had come. That is how the Rosetta Stone was secretly given to the British.

The next morning, Colonel Turner left Alexandria on a ship headed for London, England. On the ship, still covered with cloth, was the Rosetta Stone. It was the last item that the British checked off their list of treasures.

In London, Colonel Turner took the Rosetta Stone to the Society of Antiquities. The experts there made plaster casts, or copies, of the stone. To make the cast, the stone was laid on its back on a table and covered with grease or oil. Then experts covered the whole stone with a white liquid paste. The paste was pushed into the carved marks where the priest had carved the three messages many years before.

Many copies of the casts of the Rosetta Stone were made and sent to great universities all over Europe. The hope was that scientists could study the stone and learn how to read the words that were written in hieroglyphics and demotic.

Finally, the Rosetta Stone was sent to the British Museum in London to be studied. To this day, the famous black stone is there for anyone to see.

However, the story of how the code was broken is what made it so famous. Breaking the code made it possible for people everywhere to know the story of one of the greatest civilizations of all time.

Chapter 7

With the Rosetta Stone in England and copies of it available in many places of study, the hard work of trying to understand the three messages began.

A language that is written with an alphabet needs letters to spell words that people understand. If someone can speak the language, it is easier to understand the words. Since no one spoke the language of ancient Egypt, how could the demotic or hieroglyphic writing make sense?

In the early 1800s, several men worked at the same time to answer this important question. They were all very smart and had studied many different sciences. Most of them spoke more than one language and also could read and write several different languages.

All of them wanted to find out how to read the ancient language of the Egyptians so that they could learn more about life in those ancient times. They knew that the country's history was there on the walls of the old buildings, in the rolls of ancient papers, and in the books written so many years ago. The mystery was the language used to tell these stories. They needed a clue to learn how to read the information kept secret by this ancient language.

One by one, the clues were discovered. The first clue had to do with names. A researcher named the Baron de Sacey noticed that when a name was used in hieroglyphics, it was put inside a long circle with a line at one of the ends or the bottom. It looked like this ▭ or this ▭ or this ‖ .

The Baron called these long circles *cartouches* (kar-TOOSH-ez). *Cartouche* is French for the word *cartridge*. He called them that because he thought they looked like the ammunition cartridges of a rifle.

The name *Ptolemy* was the most common name used on the Rosetta Stone. The name *Cleopatra* was also used often. When the Baron de Sacey thought about the names *Ptolemy* and *Cleopatra*, he noticed something. The first letter in Ptolemy (*P*) is the fifth letter in Cleopatra (*P*). If the hieroglyphic alphabet worked, the first sign in Ptolemy would be the same as the fifth sign in Cleopatra. He discovered that it *was* the same. This was one good clue. By looking at just the names of people written in Greek, several letters could be found in the hieroglyphics.

Once the scientists found the letters of some names, they could figure out other names. One of the most famous Pharaohs of ancient Egypt was named Rameses (RAM-eh-seez). When they identified the letters *r, a,* and *s,* they could figure out that the letter *m* was missing from the name *Rameses*. In that way, they discovered the letter *m* and added it to their list of known hieroglyphic letters. Soon, with the work of two other very smart men, the alphabet was well on its way to being complete.

In England, a young man named Thomas Young studied the Rosetta Stone. He made many interesting discoveries. He was actually the first person to put the names of Cleopatra and Ptolemy together to study them. This was in 1821.

In France, Jean Francois Champollion (sham-po-YOHN) made great discoveries. Part of the reason that Champollion

learned so much was that he could speak, read, and write Coptic. Coptic is the language that is most like ancient Egyptian.

Artist's rendering by Fujiko

Champollion made great discoveries about the Rosetta Stone.

Other clues

42

were harder to figure out. Many people thought that hieroglyphics and demotic were not alphabetic. They thought they were symbols. The truth was, the writings were *both* alphabetic and symbolic.

That is not unusual. The English alphabet uses mostly letters. However, some symbols are used in writing. One example is the sign "&" for the word *and*. Also, the sign "$" is written for the word *dollar*.

One of the clues that the writing was not all symbols was that there were more than six hundred words in the Greek text, but there were more than sixteen hundred signs in the hieroglyphics. There were just too many signs to be equal to the Greek text.

Slowly, and with a lot of study, the hieroglyphic alphabet was figured out. Most of the work was done by Thomas Young and Jean Francois Champollion.

Young discovered that the alphabet was always used to spell the names of

Greek and foreign leaders in hieroglyphics. The older names, such as the names of the gods, used symbols. The problem then became how to check to see that they were right.

An English traveler, William John Bankes, found a large pointed monument in Egypt. He had the monument shipped to his home in England and put in his large backyard. There were two messages on the monument. One was in hieroglyphics, and the other one was in Greek.

Using his version of the hieroglyphic alphabet from the Rosetta Stone, Young was able to find the names of Ptolemy and Cleopatra on the monument at Bankes's house. He checked the names by reading them in Greek. Later, they were able to read the inscription on the monument in Bankes's backyard. The Greek alphabet, as Young discovered it, was used to translate the hieroglyphics.

Between the discoveries by Young and Champollion, the keys to reading the writings of the Egyptians had been discovered. They were able to read both the alphabet writings and the symbols of the ancient people. Because of their hard work and intelligence, we now know the meaning of the writings on Egyptian tombs, graves, buildings, and documents. The lives and history of a great ancient people were discovered!

Chapter 8

What exactly was the message on the Rosetta Stone? The message tells us a little about the life of the average ancient Egyptian. The message tells of a time when the human rulers of Egypt were thought to be gods.

When Ptolemy V became the king, he was very young. His mother and father were already dead. For many years, he was not only a boy but ruled as a king, too. In the year 188 B.C., after Ptolemy V's rule, a group of priests met in the city of Memphis in Egypt. They wrote a message to tell about what had happened while Ptolemy V was the king of Egypt. That is the message written on the Rosetta Stone.

The message is a thank-you note that

tells about what Ptolemy V did for the priests and the people of Egypt. The message describes how Ptolemy V was to be honored as a god. The last part of the message says that this message must be written on stone and put into the temples in all of Egypt.

King Ptolemy V, the message says, was very helpful to the people who lived in the temples of the Egyptian gods. Most of these people were priests. The message also said that Ptolemy V was a god because his dead family members were gods.

Ptolemy V was thanked because he gave tax money to the temples and gave his own money to the priests. He also said that the priests did not have to pay some taxes and that they could pay lower taxes than other people.

The message on the stone also thanked Ptolemy V because he let people out of prison. These were people who had been in prison for a long time and who had not had a trial.

Ptolemy V was thanked because he did not raise the fee to become a priest. He also said that the priests did not have to travel to Alexandria each year. (This trip was difficult for the priests who lived a long way from Alexandria.) He also lowered the taxes that the temples had to pay on cloth. Temples spent a lot of money on clean, white cloth.

The message on the Rosetta Stone thanked Ptolemy V for bringing back many of the traditions of the old Egyptian religion. He gave money for shrines to the gods and money to celebrate festivals. He gave money to rebuild temples and to make them look good.

According to the message, Ptolemy V was very good to the men who had been soldiers in the Egyptian army. He also stopped the law that forced some men to be in the navy. He protected the country from enemies and the temples from thieves. Because Ptolemy V did all of these things, the gods were good to him.

He was healthy, had many victories, and was powerful. The message said his children would be kings forever and that the priests of the temples would honor an image of him three times each day. The statue of Ptolemy V would have a special crown.

The message also said there would be a celebration in the temples on his birthday and on the day he became king. There would also be a five-day celebration every year in his honor. During the celebration, priests would wear special clothes and have special celebrations and prayers to remember the great king. The message also said that people could have private shrines in their homes to celebrate Ptolemy V and to pray to him as a god.

Then the message said that these words should be written in hieroglyphics, demotic, and Greek, all on a hard stone. The stone should be put into the temples of the first, second, and third rank. The stones should stand next to a statue of the great King Ptolemy V.

These words of honor to one man helped all of the people in the world to learn about the lives of the past. The honors the Egyptians gave him were not as important as the way that the words were used later.

There are still many languages that modern linguists (people who study languages) have not read. Even today, the writings of the Maya civilization cannot yet be completely read or understood. There is no Rosetta Stone for this language that tells the same story in two languages. This is just one example. There are still many mysteries of languages to be solved.

Chapter 9

Because of the hard work of such men as Young and Champollion, people began to understand hieroglyphics. They were able to sound out the words in the writings of the ancient Egyptians. Linguists made charts that showed how the marks in Egyptian writing sounded in modern languages. For example, they could show that the symbol ➤ would sound like an "S" in English because it represented the same sound in ancient Egyptian.

Soon people could read the sounds of hieroglyphics. They could say the words even if they did not know what the words meant.

On pages 55-57, there is a chart of Egyptian writing and the sounds the words make in English. The chart can be used two ways. First, it can tell us the sound that the Egyptian writing makes. Second, the chart can tell us what symbol is used to represent the same sound in English.

There were some sounds in the Egyptian language that do not exist in modern English. There are sounds in English that did not exist in ancient Egyptian. To write in hieroglyphics, we need to look for symbols that represent sounds in the language we speak now.

For instance, the sound of "S" and the sound of a soft "C" in English are the same. To write the Egyptian hieroglyph for that sound, we use the symbol ➡ for both "S" and "C." That shows the sound we hear.

Some sounds in English did not exist at all in ancient Egyptian. The sound we use for "V" was not an Egyptian sound. Therefore, there is no symbol for that sound. The symbol ➡ stands for the sound of "F." "F" is close to the sound of "V." We can use the symbol ![symbol] for both the English "V" and the English "F."

For practice in using the chart, try to find the sound that is represented when the symbol ![symbol] is written.

For more of a challenge, find the symbol that stands for the sound of "F" as in the first sound in the word *frog*. Then find the symbols for the rest of the letters in *frog*.

Chapter 10

Using the chart that begins on the next page, you can read some names written in hieroglyphics. Work carefully and try hard. Remember, there are several things to keep in mind that will make it easier:

- The letters in a cartouche can be read from top to bottom, from right to left, or from left to right.

- The line in the cartouche tells you the direction to read. If the line is at the bottom, start from the top and read down. If the line is at the right side of the cartouche, read from the left. If the line is at the left side of the cartouche, read from the right. You might think of the line as a stop sign. Start at the opposite direction of the line and stop when you come to it.

- Some sounds in English do not exist in ancient Egyptian. Look for sounds that are almost the same as English. "F" and "V" are close.

- A man's name will have the symbol ![man symbol] at the end of the cartouche.

- A woman's name will have the ![woman symbol] symbol at the end of the cartouche.

The Egyptian Alphabet

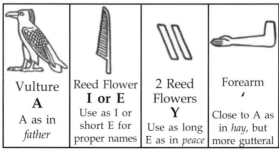

Vulture **A** A as in *father*	Reed Flower **I or E** Use as I or short E for proper names	2 Reed Flowers **Y** Use as long E as in *peace*	Forearm ′ Close to A as in *hay*, but more gutteral

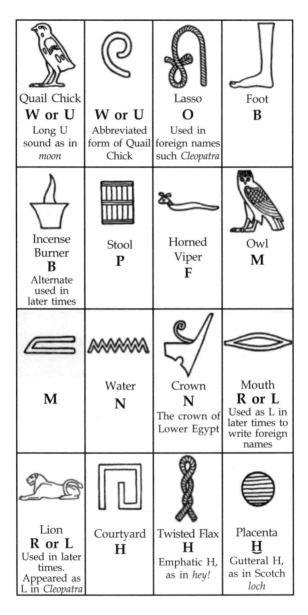

Quail Chick **W or U** Long U sound as in *moon*	**W or U** Abbreviated form of Quail Chick	Lasso **O** Used in foreign names such *Cleopatra*	Foot **B**
Incense Burner **B** Alternate used in later times	Stool **P**	Horned Viper **F**	Owl **M**
M	Water **N**	Crown **N** The crown of Lower Egypt	Mouth **R or L** Used as L in later times to write foreign names
Lion **R or L** Used in later times. Appeared as L in *Cleopatra*	Courtyard **H**	Twisted Flax **H** Emphatic H, as in *hey!*	Placenta **H̱** Gutteral H, as in Scotch *loch*

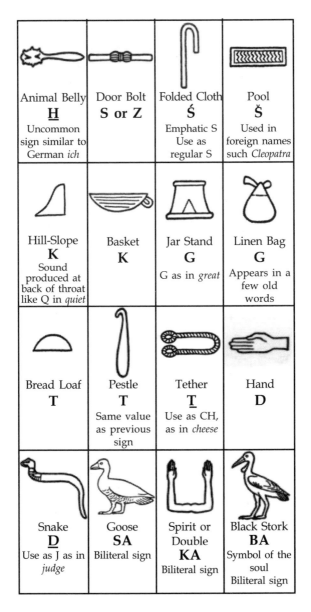			
Animal Belly **Ḥ** Uncommon sign similar to German *ich*	Door Bolt **S or Z**	Folded Cloth **Ś** Emphatic S Use as regular S	Pool **Š** Used in foreign names such *Cleopatra*
Hill-Slope **K** Sound produced at back of throat like Q in *quiet*	Basket **K**	Jar Stand **G** G as in *great*	Linen Bag **G** Appears in a few old words
Bread Loaf **T**	Pestle **T** Same value as previous sign	Tether **Ṯ** Use as CH, as in *cheese*	Hand **D**
Snake **Ḏ** Use as J as in *judge*	Goose **SA** Biliteral sign	Spirit or Double **KA** Biliteral sign	Black Stork **BA** Symbol of the soul Biliteral sign

How to Write in Hieroglyphs

Hieroglyphic writing was used in Egypt for 3,400 years. Egyptian picture writing is not easy to learn. The shapes of birds are the hardest of all to draw, but they were hard for Egyptian scribes and artists to learn, too.

Here are some helpful hints for drawing difficult signs:

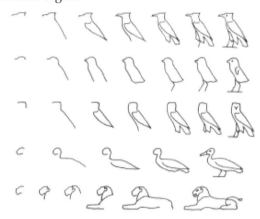

This is how the alphabet should look in handwritten form:

You'll need two more signs to write personal names. They are added at the end:

Woman   Handwritten   Man   Handwritten
Form   Form

Hieroglyphs can also be written in different directions. Here is the name *Samantha* written four ways:

Top to bottom

Left to right

Right to left

Where possible, the Egyptians liked to group the signs in boxes:

Not

When writing names in Egyptian, two points must be remembered:

1. No double letters, such as the extra **n** in **Donna**
2. No silent letters, such as the **h** in **Sarah**

Look carefully at the spelling and arrangement of the hieroglyphs in the names below:

Notice that the names are spelled by their sounds. In addition, it is possible to spell most names several different ways--experiment!

Decode the Hieroglyphs

Copy these sample hieroglyphs onto a plain piece of paper and try to break the code.

1.

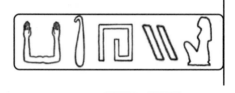

_____

2.

_____

3.

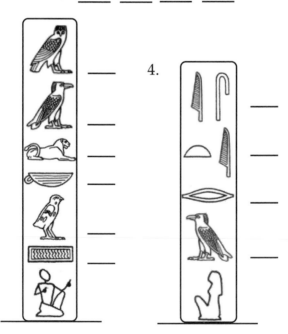

4.

Draw the Hieroglyphs

Use a separate piece of paper.

1.

___E___ ___S___ ___O___ ___J___

2.

___R___ ___Y___ ___A___ ___N___

3.

___J___

___A___

___Z___

___M___

___I___

___N___

4.

___SA___

___B___

___R___

___I___

___N___

___A___

Answers

Page 60
1. Ricardo
2. Kathy
3. Marcus
4. Estela

Page 61 *(answers may vary)*

1.

2.
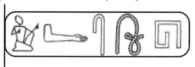

3.
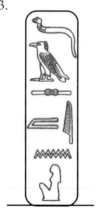

4.
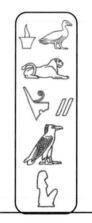

Bibliography

Andrews, Carol. *The British Museum Book of the Rosetta Stone*. New York: P. Bedrick, 1985.

Budge, E. A. Wallis. *The Rosetta Stone*. London: British Museum, 1950.

Budge, E. A. Wallis. *The Rosetta Stone in the British Museum*. New York: Dover Publications, 1989.

Donoughue, Carol. *The Mystery of the Hieroglyphs: the Story of the Rosetta Stone and the Race to Decipher Egyptian Hieroglyphs*. New York: Oxford, 2001.

Giblin, James. *The Riddle of the Rosetta Stone*. New York: Harper Trophy, 1992.

Parkinson, R. B. *Cracking Codes: The Rosetta Stone and Decipherment*. Berkley: University of California Press, 1999.

Other Nonfiction Read-Along

Disasters

- Challenger
- The Kuwaiti Oil Fires
- The Last Flight of 007
- The Mount St. Helens Volcano
- The Nuclear Disaster at Chernobyl

Disaster Display Set (5 each of 5 titles 25 books in all)
80106

Natural Disasters

- Blizzards
- Earthquakes
- Hurricanes and Floods
- Tornadoes
- Wildfires

Disaster Display Set (5 each of 5 titles 25 books in all)
80032

www.artesianpress.com